THE JOURNEY WITHIN

Learning to
Live the
Holy Life

FRANK MOORE

The *Holy Life* Bible Study Series

BOOK 2

Beacon Hill Press of Kansas City
Kansas City, Missouri

Copyright 2004
by Frank Moore and
Beacon Hill Press of Kansas City

ISBN 083-412-1107

Printed in the
United States of America

Cover Design: Ted Ferguson

Library of Congress Cataloging-in-Publication Data
Moore, Frank, 1951-
    The journey within : learning to live the holy life / Frank Moore.
        p. cm. — (The holy life Bible study series ; bk. 2)
    ISBN 0-8341-2110-7 (pbk.)
    1. Holiness. 2. Holiness—Biblical teaching. I. Title II. Moore, Frank, 1951- .
Holy life Bible study series ; bk. 2.

    BT767.M6745 2004
    248.4'071—dc22

                                                    2004003068

10 9 8 7 6 5 4 3 2 1

Contents

For the Group Leader

How to Use This Study Book

We trust that this study will be a valuable resource to you and others in helping you grow in holiness and Christlikeness. It is written and organized to be used as a small-group Bible study, with 12 weekly sessions. The following are some brief guidelines to help you maximize your group's time together.

1. Pray regularly throughout the week that your group sessions will be times of warm fellowship and genuine spiritual growth. Most of all, ask that the Holy Spirit will be present in a powerful way, speaking to and challenging each group member to a life of holiness. Open and close each weekly session in prayer.

2. Prepare well for each session. Carefully study the scripture readings and exposition prior to your group meeting, which will help you facilitate the discussions and keep them moving.

3. Use the group discussion questions and activities to promote lively dialogue among group members. Feel free to contribute your own comments as well, but don't allow any one member of the group (including *yourself*) to dominate the discussions.

4. Whenever it's practical, link your own comments to those of others. Affirm each group member. This will help encourage some of the more reticent members of your group to participate in the discussions.

5. Respect confidentiality within the group.

6. Encourage group members to come to each session prepared, having studied the lesson carefully, and having meditated on the personal reflection questions.

7. Encourage any group member who has made any type of personal decision for Christ (salvation, sanctification, or other) to make his or her decision public as soon as possible at one of your church's worship services.

New Testament Snapshots of Holiness

Luke 1:74-75; Matt. 5:48; 2 Cor. 7:1; Eph. 4:22-24

In Book 1 of this Bible study series, we looked at God's original plan for humanity, humanity's rejection of that plan, and His efforts at getting us back on track with the plan—not for the sake of the plan but for the sake of our relationship with Him. His desire for relationship with us springs not so much because He needs us but rather because we need Him. We don't know it or acknowledge it prior to becoming Christians, but more than anything else in the world, we need relationship with God.

Most of the scripture studies in Book 1 focused on Old Testament passages. Even the New Testament passages we considered referred to concepts from the Old Testament. Now our attention primarily shifts to studies in the New Testament. Does the New Testament portray God maintaining a desire for our holiness, or does He drop the idea as a notion whose time has passed? As we look to the New Testament, we see that God desires more than ever that we live holy lives. Rather than decreasing this emphasis, He actually increases it to include even more facets of our lives.

This first study in Book 2 focuses attention on a variety of scriptures throughout the New Testament, giving us a holiness snapshot found in the new covenant.

READ LUKE 1:74-75

John the Baptist paved the way for Jesus' coming. Almost everything about his life was unusual: his diet, his manner of dress, and even his birth to godly, elderly parents. Zechariah, John's father, declared the word of the Lord in a special message of prophecy spoken at John's dedication ceremony. We find Zechariah's dedication message for John in Luke 1:68-79. He saw the ministry that lay ahead for his son, one that would prepare the way for the coming Messiah.

In this prophecy Zechariah spoke of the deliverance and salvation of God's people. Notice the focus of verses 74-75. He said the Messiah would rescue us from our enemies and enable us to serve God without fear. We would be empowered to do this in holiness and righteousness. In other words, our actions as well as our heart motives and intentions can be correct in God's eyes.

When will we be enabled to do this? Is it after we die and go to heaven? Is it at the end of our lives on earth? No, the Messiah will enable us to live in holiness and righteousness before Him "all our days." So from the time we accept the good news of the gospel message and believe in Jesus Christ as personal Savior, we can become new creatures who please God in both action and attitude.

GROUP DISCUSSION

1. Why did God tell us about the Messiah's provision of holiness and righteousness for our lives prior to His coming?

2. Does this prophecy leave any question regarding God's intention for our lives once we accept His Messiah?

3. From God's perspective, does our holiness appear to be a fanciful hope or an emerging reality?

READ MATT. 5:48

The Sermon on the Mount is perhaps the best-known sermon from the earthly ministry of Jesus Christ. Recorded in Matt. 5—7, this sermon summarizes the ethical teachings of Jesus' ministry. Jesus covers the waterfront in this sermon of how we are to live toward God, other people, and ourselves. He offers directives on everything from getting along with family members to enjoying a meaningful prayer life.

Planted in the middle of this sermon is one of the most powerful admonitions in the entire ministry of Jesus. He calls on us to "be perfect, therefore, as your heavenly Father is perfect." What does that mean? How perfect are you feeling today? Perfect enough to compare yourself with God? Not likely. And yet we can't just dismiss this admonition as a lofty yet unattainable goal. God's not one to dangle a carrot on a string just out of our reach and urge us to reach toward what He knows we can never grasp. His goals for our lives are far more realistic than that. So it's not likely that Jesus is commanding an unrealistic expectation.

What if Jesus is not even giving a command here? What if He's making us a promise? Now that throws a different light on the verse, doesn't it? Maybe Jesus is saying that when we love God and other people the way He described in verses 43-47, and when we give to the needy, pray, fast, preference Kingdom values as He describes later in chapter 6, then we are perfect as God is perfect!

If this verse is a promise rather than a command, Jesus is not requiring our divine perfection in performance. He is saying God looks at and takes into consideration our hearts, our intentions, our motives, and our desires. As elsewhere in the Sermon on the Mount, in this verse Jesus calls for a heart centered on putting God and *His* values first.

PERSONAL REFLECTION

1. Have you read this verse in the past?

2. If so, how did you feel about attempting to apply it to your life?

3. How does it change your response if Jesus' statement is making a promise rather than giving a command?

4. Why does God place so much emphasis on our intentions, motives, and desires rather than simply our actions?

READ 2 COR. 7:1

The "since" that begins this verse refers back to Paul's discussion regarding not being yoked with unbelievers. He's referencing an Old Testament thought such as is found in Deut. 22:9-11 about not mixing different things together, such as combining different kinds of seeds in your garden, yoking an ox with a donkey, or wearing clothes made of different types of cloth. Paul sees no place for believers to join with false teachers who speak for Satan.

This leads Paul to the conclusion that we Christians have the responsibility to purify ourselves. What does he mean by this? Is Paul calling for us to make ourselves divine or performance-perfect? No. He's telling us to drop everything in our lives that we know wars spiritually against our bodies or spirits. Get rid of everything that tries to compromise our commitments to Christ. We must not yoke ourselves with anything that weakens our bond to God or threatens our relationships with Him.

GROUP DISCUSSION

1. Give examples of things that contaminate our bodies.

2. Give examples of things that contaminate our spirits.

3. Can we reach a compromise with some of these impediments to our faith or relationships with God and keep them in our lives while we serve God? Why or why not?

4. Is Paul's call for us to perfect holiness in our lives a realistic one? In other words, is the goal attainable or unattainable?

READ EPH. 4:22-24

Paul calls us to a standard similar to what Jesus urged upon us in Matt. 5:48, that is, to be righteous and holy like God. He offers us this goal and also presents a plan to accomplish it. He reminds us that when we received the gift of God's grace for the forgiveness of our sins, we took off the old clothes of our sinful lifestyle. Once adopted into the family of God, we put on the new clothes that Christ gave us. The forgiveness, the adoption, and the new clothes all came our way as free gifts of God's grace. We now have a responsibility to constantly remind ourselves of that fact and live consistently in Christ.

Paul is not calling us to earn our salvation through works. Rather, the lifestyle of righteousness and holiness follow naturally as fruit in a believer who keeps his or her mind focused on Christ and wears the new clothes of Christ every day. This daily practice moves us to lives that not only please God but also make us *like* God. What a powerful thought!

GROUP DISCUSSION

1. Give examples of the "old clothes" we take off when we become Christians.

2. Give examples of the "new clothes" we put on when we become Christians.

GROUP ACTIVITY

Select four individuals from the Bible study group to serve in a panel discussion. Ask each to select a passage of Scripture from this week's lesson and explain why it's important.

FOR FURTHER STUDY

Along with the scriptures considered in this Bible study, see also the following ones:
1 Pet. 1:15-16; 2 Pet. 3:11; Heb. 12:14

Another Counselor

John 14:15-18, 26-27; 15:26-27; 16:7-11, 13-14

People often search for the distinctive feature of Christianity that sets it apart from other religions of the world. All religions have a founder. Most have a significant leader. Many have a sacred text. All followers pray in one form or another to a supreme being. However, Christianity stands alone with one unique and significant feature: Christians communicate with God on a two-way street. They enjoy a relationship, a fellowship, even a love affair with God.

How is that possible? It's by the ministry of the Holy Spirit, who speaks the words of God—not to our ears but to our hearts and minds. He brings the presence of God to our inner beings in a way more profound than words can adequately describe.

PERSONAL REFLECTION

Stop for a minute and consider how meaningful your faith would be to you if your prayers were only a one-way street and you did all the talking. Imagine never hearing the words of God in your heart. Imagine religion only as a human effort.

1. How meaningful would your faith be?

2. How helpful would prayer be?

3. How much spiritual confidence would such a religion give you?

GROUP ACTIVITY

Group leader: Give every Bible study participant a small piece of red construction paper. Tell class members to interrupt you by waving their red "flags" every time you make an incorrect statement in your presentation. If they interrupt your lecture, they must then correct the incorrect statement. Then, as you make your Bible study presentation, purposefully make incorrect statements to see if class members correct you. If they miss something important, stop and correct your own statement. This activity will keep everyone listening and makes participation lively.

Most of what we know about the Holy Spirit comes to us from the words of Jesus. Our Bible lessons for today provide foundation for what are known as the five Paraclete sayings of Jesus. *Paraclete* is a Greek word meaning "one called alongside." It images a Comforter, Counselor, Advocate, or Helper.

READ JOHN 14:15-16

Jesus, our first Counselor, tells us here about "another Counselor" who will bring us the presence of the living Christ. Christ is the very essence of truth, because God defines truth. Lies and deception fill our world, but God always represents truth. Notice the use of the words "with" and "in" in verse 17. The Spirit who had been living with Jesus' disciples would relocate himself to live in their hearts. What a powerful notion! What could be better than having the One who defines truth as a permanent heart guest? Jesus promises to rise from the dead and return to earth at the end of time in great glory. Until then, His Holy Spirit will abide in us.

GROUP DISCUSSION

1. Why do people pay their hard-earned money to get the advice and direction of professional counselors?

2. What do professional counselors offer that well-meaning friends might not have to give?

3. In what ways is the Holy Spirit better than a professional counselor?

4. In what ways is "the other Counselor" (Holy Spirit) like "the first Counselor" (Jesus)?

READ JOHN 14:26-27

The gospels teem with the teachings, sayings, and parables of Jesus. He gave us too much to digest on our own. One of the most amazing features of the Bible is its power to instruct us whether we're reading a passage for the first time or the 100th time. Every reading sounds like Jesus speaking the words for the first time. That's because the Holy Spirit instructs us as we read. We're not just reading words on a page —we're receiving instruction from God himself. What's more, the Spirit remains faithful to remind us of previous lessons He's already taught us that we've let slip from our minds. A lifetime of Bible study will never exhaust the teaching and re-teaching ministry of the Holy Spirit.

GROUP DISCUSSION

1. What other world religions offer personal tutoring by the creator of the universe?

2. How does the Holy Spirit communicate with your heart?

3. Why do we need the Holy Spirit's teaching and reteaching ministry?

4. What is the connection between the teaching ministry of the Holy Spirit and the peace of heart that God gives?

READ JOHN 15:26-27

The Holy Spirit conducts a powerful work of witnessing to the world about the life, ministry, and salvation of Jesus Christ. The Spirit of Truth bears witness to the Truth. Sometimes we think of witnessing for Christ as a work that we do. It is and it isn't. Yes, we tell others what Christ has done in our lives. No, we don't do it by our own strength, power, or ability. We're able to successfully witness for Christ as "the Witness" works in us and empowers us.

GROUP DISCUSSION

1. What's the easiest part of witnessing for Christ?

2. What's the hardest part of witnessing for Christ?

3. What role do you allow the Holy Spirit to play in your personal witness?

4. How could you better make yourself available to His ministry of witness in you?

READ JOHN 16:7-11

Most of us who call ourselves Christians first learned about the ministry of the Holy Spirit at the time of our conversion or shortly thereafter. We weren't aware of the fact that long before we accepted Christ as our personal Savior, the Holy Spirit brought conviction to our hearts. We woke up to the reality of our sinfulness and our need for God's help. We knew that our actions as well as many of the desires of our hearts were sinful. The Holy Spirit brought us to a crisis point of decision. He called for an answer to the haunting question "What will you do with Jesus?"

What the Holy Spirit did for us He does for every man, woman, boy, and girl on this earth. He talks to everyone about his or her personal sins. He places a haunting desire in the soul of every person to live a righteous life. He won't let us go to sleep at night or think sobering thoughts without reminding us of the coming judgment and our appearance before the Judge of all the earth. Does He make us uncomfortable with these convicting thoughts to haunt or scare us? Never. Rather, it's because He loves us too much to let us live without a relationship with God.

PERSONAL REFLECTION

1. Think of a time when you felt God's conviction. How did God's conviction feel?

2. What did it make you want to do, run from or toward God?

3. What did you do?

4. What lessons do you learn about God from the Spirit's convicting ministry?

5. How can you tell when a friend is experiencing God's conviction?

READ JOHN 16:13-14

We live in a day of moral pluralism, relativism, and subjectivism. Our culture tells us that we can't state anything as a certain fact—it's all relative. What works for you is right for you; what works for me is right for me. This way of seeing life splits truth into a thousand pieces to be interpreted by a thousand different people. As someone said to me, "Truth is whatever I want it to be." Not so. This passage of Scripture reminds us that God's definition of truth differs from the definition of our postmodern world.

The Spirit of God is the Spirit of Truth, and He will willingly guide into objective truth all who seek Him—not the lofty thoughts of humanity, mind you, but the Truth from the One who defines truth by His very nature. Notice how closely the members of the Trinity work together. None ministers to us independent of the other. All work together to bring us to certain knowledge of God's truth—a truth that will set us free (John 8:32).

God even goes so far as to tell us of things yet to come. Some think this refers to God's revealing future events to us ahead of time, as He sometimes did with certain Bible characters. However, it may refer to God preparing us for what lies ahead in each new day of our Christian lives. With this preparation, we're ready for whatever comes our way on any given day.

GROUP DISCUSSION

1. Why are moral pluralism, relativism, and subjectivism so popular in modern culture?

2. Give examples of moral pluralism, relativism, and subjectivism in your world.

3. Why are moral pluralism, relativism, and subjectivism such enemies to God's objective truth?

4. What are the advantages to defining your own truth?

5. What are the disadvantages to defining your own truth?

6. What happens to us if we choose culture's definition of truth over God's definition?

CONCLUSION

There you have it: another counselor, this one working from within your heart.

1. What does God's Spirit do for you on a daily basis?

2. Why does He go to so much effort in your life?

4. In what ways could you open yourself more fully to the ministry of the Holy Spirit?

FOR FURTHER STUDY

Matt. 28:18-19; John 1:32-33; John 8:32; John 20:21-22; Rom. 8:11; 1 John 1:5—2:6

A Big Event for Your Big Adventure

Acts 1:4-8; 2:1-4

From time to time, famous movie stars in Hollywood or political figures in Washington, D.C., host large parties. They spare no expense as food and drink flow in abundance. Music fills the air. Balloons and decorations announce a celebration. News commentators occasionally remark, "These folks know how to signal a big event."

However, no party planner in Hollywood or Washington even comes close to some of God's "big events." The parting of the Red Sea (Exod. 14:15-31), the extension of a day (Josh. 10:12-14), and the fire and thunder at the giving of the Ten Commandments (Exod. 19:16-19) all amazed those who experienced them. This session's Scripture lesson tells of God's festive celebration at the birthday of the Church. People have been talking about that day for nearly 2,000 years; what God did for His disciples that day He's been doing for His other children to this very day.

GROUP DISCUSSION

Think of a big event of which you've seen pictures in the news.

1. What did the event commemorate?

2. How many people experienced it firsthand?

3. What made the event spectacular?

4. How do God's big events in the Bible differ from the ones we see in the news today?

READ ACTS 1:4-5

Jesus' disciples rode the emotional roller coaster of His last days of ministry, His crucifixion, His resurrection, and His parting words. As they said their last good-byes together, Jesus left His disciples a promise. He had told them about the Holy Spirit prior to His crucifixion (John 14—17). Now the time had arrived for them to meet Him personally. Jesus compared the Holy Spirit's coming to a baptism, something like the water baptism of John the Baptist (Matt. 3:11-12). John preached a message of repentance. The Spirit's baptism would result in a heart cleansing. Both baptisms are important; the Spirit's is superior to John's.

GROUP DISCUSSION

1. Why did Jesus not satisfy the curiosity of His disciples about the coming of the Holy Spirit?

2. Why did He leave them with more questions than answers?

3. Why does God often accomplish His purposes (like bringing about His kingdom) with unlikely means (such as the disciples' witness)?

4. Think of other examples in the Bible in which God accomplished His purposes with unlikely means.

Jesus set the bar of anticipation high as He talked about such things as power, being internally filled with the Holy Spirit, and being witnesses of Christ all over the world. The power He talked about in verse 8 differed greatly from the power they inferred in verse 6. The disciples hoped Jesus would exercise political power; He envisioned spiritual power for His followers. His kingdom would come, all right, but not through a political revolution. His plan was far more subtle; He would bring about His kingdom through the disciples' personal witness given in the power of the Holy Spirit.

The disciples couldn't grasp Jesus' big vision. They honestly had no idea of what He was talking about. They could tell from His description, however, that this baptism would be absolutely essential for their success with the mission He had given them to tackle once He left them (Matt. 28:19-20). No doubt, fear and uncertainty gripped their hearts at that moment. Jesus assured them that the Spirit's presence would make them adequate for the task.

PERSONAL REFLECTION

1. Put yourself in Jesus' disciples' sandals. How might you have felt following more than 40 days of emotional ups and downs surrounding the events of Jesus' life?

2. What would have been your reaction to the anxious anticipation Jesus created with His call to wait and His promise
   of a new baptism?

3. Do you think you would have grasped the vision of Jesus
   any better than His disciples grasped it that day?

READ ACTS 2:1-4

The birthday of the Church occurred on the Feast of Pentecost. This was no coincidence, just as Jesus' crucifixion at
the Feast of Passover had been no coincidence. The timing of
both events holds great significance in biblical and spiritual
symbolism.

The Feast of Passover commemorated the Hebrew people's exodus from Egyptian bondage (Exod. 12:41-43). The
death of Jesus brought the possibility for humanity's deliverance from sin's bondage. The Feast of Pentecost commemorated God's giving the Hebrew people His law (Lev. 23:15-
16). The coming of the Holy Spirit brought us the internal
power and ability to live the way the law originally intended
for us to live.

Isn't it amazing how God works to teach us spiritual truths
even in the timing of events like Christ's death and the Holy
Spirit's coming?

GROUP DISCUSSION

1. What spiritual significance do you see between the Hebrew people's exodus from Egyptian bondage and Jesus' death on the Cross?

2. What spiritual significance do you see between God's giving the Hebrew people His law and His giving the Early Church His Holy Spirit?

The connection between the giving of the law in the Old Testament and the coming of the Holy Spirit in the New Testament does not end with timing. God's announcement of a spectacular event with bright light and loud sounds accompanied both. At the giving of the law, God used thunder, lightning, a thick cloud, and a very loud trumpet blast (Exod. 19:16). At the coming of the Holy Spirit, God used a blast of wind, individual flames of fire, and a miraculous ability for Jesus' disciples to speak in languages they had never learned.

Each of the three symbols God used at the Spirit's coming signified spiritual meaning. The wind reminds us of its ability to separate chaff from wheat (Matt. 3:12). The Spirit comes to blow away all that's unholy in our lives. The flames of fire remind us of their ability to burn chaff and purge gold and silver from their impurities (Mal. 3:2-4). The Spirit comes to purge our hearts of all that makes us less than God hopes for us to be. The miracle of languages reminds us of the call to communicate the Good News of Jesus Christ to every person in his or her own tongue (Matt. 28:19-20).

GROUP DISCUSSION

1. Why does God often use unusual means to announce spectacular events?

2. What kinds of things does the Spirit's wind blow away from our lives?

3. What kinds of things does the Spirit's fire burn up or purge from our hearts?

4. How do we fulfill our continuing responsibility to take the good news of Jesus Christ to every person in every language group?

The worst part of a big event? The cleanup aftermath! Sometimes we're left with quite a mess. After the balloons and streamers are taken down, the trash gathered, and the place swept, we often look back on the scene and ask, "What really happened here?" We're looking for the continuing results or the long-term effect of the big event.

This same question can be asked about the Day of Pentecost in the lives of Jesus' disciples after the wind ceased, the fire died, and the spoken word fell silent. The Book of Acts tells the rest of the story: the gospel message began to spread across the entire world. Pentecost was more than a birthday celebration for the emerging Church. Disciples sprang up everywhere. The results lasted far beyond clean-up day. Pentecost launched a revolution in the hearts of Jesus' disciples both then and now. The power of which Jesus spoke in Acts 1:8 changed forever the way God grows His kingdom.

PERSONAL REFLECTION

Reflect on the sights and sounds of the Day of Pentecost as described in Acts 2:1-4.

Why do today's disciples of Christ still need a Pentecost-like event in their lives to prepare them for God's big adventure?

GROUP ACTIVITY

This study emphasized God's use of symbols to instruct us. Give each member of your Bible study group a lump of Play-doh. Have everyone mold something that symbolizes God's work in his or her life and then share the spiritual insight of his or her symbol.

FOR FURTHER STUDY

Acts 2:37-29; Acts 8:1-40; Acts 10:1-48

FURTHER QUESTIONS

Take a moment at the conclusion of the session to encourage class participants to place their unanswered questions on note cards, along with this session number. They should then place their cards in an "odds and ends" box provided by the Bible study leader. Attention will be given to these questions in the last session of this study.

A Call to Holiness

Rom. 6:6-18

My house has several outside doors that all lead inside. The front of the house has the biggest door. But you can also enter the house from two side doors and three back doors. Each door brings you into a different room. Once inside, however, you can explore the entire building.

That's like the Bible's call to holiness. The New Testament offers us a number of entry points for studying it. All of them offer helpful insights. Any one of them will get us into the subject and allow us to explore God's gift to us. Let's jump in at Rom. 6 and begin our exploration.

READ ROM. 6:6-10

Like running to catch up to a slow-moving train, we need to catch up to Paul's thought starting in verse 6. He begins this train of thought in 5:1 when he reminds us that God's grace justified us through faith. God cancelled our past lives of sin and deleted the record. He could do this for us because of Christ's death on the Cross.

Beginning at 5:9, Paul switches gears and unfolds the practical implication of this free grace, that is, holy living. The old life of sinning vanishes. We never return to it even for a brief visit (6:1). Baptism offers Paul an illustration. We bury our old lives with Christ in the water grave of baptism. We spring forth from the water just as Christ sprung forth from the grave. We now live a new life in Christ. Holy living has begun.

Beginning in 6:6, Paul quickly recaps his developing thought. God destroys our old sinful lives. Sin dominated our unregenerate selves. Sin hung around our necks like a dead, decaying body always threatening to kill us. But Christ changed all that for us. He gave us a new set of clothes, a new way of living. Now we no longer serve the drives of our old ways or have sin hanging around our necks.

Since we've died to sin's drives, we're free from them. No longer should these drives enslave us. Sin's condemnation no longer binds us; sin's dominion no longer controls us. The standards of the law find us guilty. However, Christ announces our deliverance. Sin once held us in the throes of death; thankfully, God raised us to new life in Christ. The Resurrection power that raised Christ from the grave now works in us to break the chains of both sin and spiritual death, which bind us. God has destroyed that which threatened to destroy us.

GROUP DISCUSSION

1. In what ways did your old life of sin enslave you?

2. How did your old life threaten to destroy you?

3. How did your old way of life threaten to destroy others?

4. In what practical way is the gospel message "good news"?

5. What feelings come to mind as you contemplate God's gift of salvation to you?

READ ROM. 6:11-14

The first portion of this week's study (Rom. 6:6-10) places emphasis on what God has done for us. This portion shifts the emphasis to our responsibility as believers in Christ to put ourselves in a position to live holy lives.

Verse 11 tells us to first "count yourselves dead to sin." Like balancing your checkbook, add all of these facts up and total them. They total an awareness that your old life of sin is dead; the only life you now have comes from God. So live like it! This verse also contains the secret to this new God-life. For the first time in Romans, Paul uses his familiar formula for this secret. It's living "in Christ." In other words, we find our source of strength for daily living not in positive thinking, self-actualization, or determination. We don't pull ourselves up by our own bootstraps, slap on smiles, and grind our way through another day. We find strength for the day by living in Christ. Paul uses the phrase more than 90 times in his letters. Here are a few examples: Rom. 8:1; 1 Cor. 1:2, 4, 30; 4:17; 15:19, 22.

The second thing we do to position ourselves for holy living appears in verse 12: "do not let sin reign in your mortal body." We make choices every day to use our bodies for God's purposes and glory or for our own desires. We can't blame the devil, temptation, bad habits, past failures, or a dysfunctional family for sinful choices. We must own our actions; they are the products of our own willed desires.

The third thing we do to position ourselves for holy living appears in verse 13: "offer yourselves to God." This speaks of our consecration to God. We must take the initiative and present ourselves to Him who justifies us freely. With our consecration comes our promise to use our bodies for God's purpose and not our own.

When we do these three things—count, choose, and offer —the power of sin over us is broken. Sin's enslavement ends. God breaks the law's condemnation. The law failed us in that it only made us feel guilty. It never offered power or ability to resist sin. It only pointed out how far short we always fell. So now we offer ourselves to a new master: God's grace.

PERSONAL REFLECTION

1. Do you feel empowered now that you realize you have a part to play in applying God's grace to your life? Why or why not?

2. List some practical examples of ways you count yourself dead to sin.

3. What role do you play in controlling the physical, emotional, or psychological desires that call for your attention and demand gratification?

4. How do you offer yourself to God? What are the steps to your consecration?

READ ROM. 6:15-18

In verses 15-18 Paul answers a question raised by those seeking to understand his position. The thrust of the original language poses it this way: "Can we take a break from righteousness occasionally and sin just a little?" It's the idea of an infrequent, planned indiscretion as opposed to an ongoing lifestyle of sinfulness. Paul's response: "No way!" We are as done with sinning as a dead person is with breathing.

Paul invites us to exchange masters. It's a given fact that we will serve a master. The question is—which master will we choose to serve? As sinners we served sin and self. As believers, Paul admonishes, we're to serve God. This service manifests itself in three ways: by doing the right things (v. 16), by obeying the commands of Christ (v. 17), and by submitting voluntarily as slaves to God (v. 18).

In verse 17 Paul offers a word of praise to God that we have been delivered from sin's dominion. He mentions the source of this good news message, that is, the Christian doctrines that his readers had received and followed. Here we find another reason to involve ourselves in Bible studies such as this one. We want to know what the Bible says so we can understand correct doctrine. A truly Christian lifestyle should then follow from this understanding.

GROUP DISCUSSION

1. Why do you suppose Paul took several opportunities in Rom. 6 to address the problem of practicing a lifestyle of sin after a person becomes a Christian?

2. Why does everyone consciously or unconsciously serve a master?

3. What examples in everyday life illustrate this truth?

4. How do we know the right things to do as admonished in verse 16?

5. Where do we find Christ's commands that Paul tells us to follow in verse 17?

6. How do we demonstrate in concrete ways that we are slaves to God as described in verse 18?

CONCLUSION

In this session's passage of Scripture, Paul calls attention to our introduction into the holy life. It begins at our conversion to Christ. Becoming a new creature in Christ ushers in a changed lifestyle that is so radical it can only be described as a death (to the old) and a resurrection (to the new). Everything changes. We exchange our slavery to sin for slavery to God. As we continue to grow in this new life of holiness, God leads us naturally into a deeper walk with Him. This will be the focus of our next Bible study.

FOR FURTHER STUDY

Gal. 2:20; Gal. 3:23-25; Col. 2:20

FURTHER QUESTIONS

Take a moment at the conclusion of the session to encourage class participants to place their unanswered questions on note cards, along with this session number. They should then place their cards in an "odds and ends" box provided by the Bible study leader. Attention will be given to these questions in the last session of this study.

Needed: Heart Cleansing

Ps. 51:1-12

Studies 2 and 3 of this series introduced the ministry of the Holy Spirit in the Church and our personal lives. Because so much attention is given to the Day of Pentecost as the birthday of the Church, we tend to think of the big event of Pentecost as the beginning of the Holy Spirit's work with people. This makes sense, because the Spirit receives top billing for the spiritual direction of the Church and our lives from that day forward. Further, we tend to think the New Testament is the beginning of the call to heart purity and cleansing. Not so.

The Holy Spirit is a vital member of the Trinity, and the Trinity always works as one Person. Therefore, any time God worked in the Old Testament, you can rest assured that the Holy Spirit involved himself in some capacity. Most of the Old Testament references to God focus attention on God the Father. Our biblical study passage for today, however, focuses attention on the Holy Spirit. This is the only Old Testament study passage in this book. We studied primarily Old Testament concepts in the previous volume of this Bible study series. We inserted a study of Ps. 51 at this juncture because the concepts explored in this text make more sense after Jesus explains the Holy Spirit's ministry (John 14—17) and after the Spirit takes residence in our hearts (Acts 2).

BACKGROUND CHECK

Many Christians tend not to think of the Holy Spirit at work in the Old Testament. However, with further reflection, we see several references to His work throughout human history. Check out the following references to illustrate His involvement.
1. Gen. 1:2

2. Exod. 31:1-5
3. Judg. 3:10, 11:29, 14:6; and 15:14
4. Isa. 11:1-3; 61:1-3; and 63:10-11

GROUP DISCUSSION

What do you learn about the Holy Spirit's work in the Old Testament from reading the passages of Scripture listed above?

READ PS. 51:1-4

This psalm finds David more than a year after his adultery with Bathsheba. He's in big trouble with God and himself, and he knows it. His prayer deals with two distinct spiritual needs: (1) God's forgiveness of past sins and (2) his forgiven heart to be cleansed from the tendency to sin. We will primarily focus our attention on the second need.

The first section of material considers the need for God's forgiveness. Notice David's call for God's mercy, unfailing love, great compassion, and ability to blot transgressions from the divine record. David testifies that his sins haunt him daily. Sins always do. He states an important spiritual truth when he says that we not only hurt ourselves and innocent victims when we sin, but we also hurt God. That's the primary hurt. David has been caught red-handed in his sin, and he acknowledges that he deserves God's judgment for it.

PERSONAL REFLECTION

If you're a believer, see if you can identify with David in this passage.

1. Did you reach a point in your life at which you came face-to-face with your sins?

2. In what ways did you acknowledge your sin as David did here?

3. Did your sins haunt you as David's sins haunted him?

4. What did God do for you when you prayed to Him about your problem?

GROUP ACTIVITY

Have the Bible study leader interview a participant who has had opportunity to prepare beforehand and who is willing to share from his or her personal spiritual journey. The leader will ask interview-type questions that explore this person's realization of his or her need for heart cleansing. This exercise aims not so much to call attention to one individual's experience as to get all class members to examine their own lives with regard to this need for heart cleansing.

READ PS. 51:5-6

Verse 5 calls attention to the reason human hearts need cleansing. Unfortunately, the *New International Version* (NIV) translation of this verse obscures the original meaning. You might imply (incorrectly) from the NIV reading that we begin sinning as soon as we are born. David actually means, "Surely in iniquity I was born." In other words, we come into this world with a human nature turned inward on self. From infancy we prefer our own interests, even if they go against God's will for our lives. Human hearts need cleansing, because they're tainted with the self-sovereignty problem passed down from our original parents.

David further highlights his focus on the wellspring of our souls in verse 6 as he calls attention to our need for God to deal with our "inner parts" or our "inmost place." We never solve the problem of sinning by coming up with a longer list of rules or putting more police officers on the streets. The problem must be solved at its source, where the desire to sin begins. Once God cleanses the source, the sin problem can be solved.

GROUP DISCUSSION

1. Why are the selfish actions of babies and small children not regarded as sinful?

2. At what point do we label such actions sinful?

3. What evidence do you see in your world that every human being who lives on the face of the earth has a tendency toward self-preference or self-sovereignty?

4. Why will external measures, like rules and police officers, not solve the human nature problem?

READ PS. 51:7-12

In the first part of the prayer, David focuses attention on his act of sin. In the second part, he focuses on his human nature, which urges him to sin. Now he pleads for God's cleansing. The literal meaning of the word used here for "cleanse" is "un-sin." He calls for not just an outward or ceremonial cleansing, as with hyssop, in the forgiveness of his sinful acts. He needs a divine washing of his inner nature. David's call for two cleansings implies that he seeks a work from God that will make his heart so pure that no figure of speech or no ceremony can capture it.

Beyond the washing, he needs an inner transformation that will change him from the inside out. Only then will he get his joy, gladness, and rejoicing back. He can rejoice again only after he knows that God no longer sees the sin that David sees all too clearly.

GROUP DISCUSSION

1. How does God "un-sin" us?

2. How do you feel when you remember that God takes our sins away from us?

3. What does David's request for two cleansings imply about our spiritual need?

The focal point of this week's Bible study zeros in on verses 10-12. Here lies the heart of the matter. God's forgiveness of our sins is essential, but forgiveness is never enough. David located the source of his sin in his human nature. Now he prays for God to deal decisively with that sinful nature. This prayer for purity asks God for three things: (1) a clean heart, (2) a right spirit, and (3) a sense of God's Holy Spirit living within him. True, the ministry of the Holy Spirit in the hearts of all believers as we know it today did not come to full reality until the Day of Pentecost. And yet David hits on something here that stands out in salvation history as an important spiritual insight. In some ways, He was ahead of his time in understanding what we all need in order to solve the sin problem: *heart cleansing.*

If God renews David and if the Spirit indwells him, he will get back the joy of his salvation and a willing spirit to persevere to the end.

GROUP DISCUSSION

1. Use your own words to describe what David wants when he asks God for
   - a clean heart

   - a right spirit

   - a sense of God's Holy Spirit living within him.

2. How is it that David, who fell so deeply into sin, had such a profound spiritual insight into the true nature of his need?

3. In your own words, describe how you have come to realize your personal need for heart cleansing.

4. In what ways have you prayed for a willing spirit to persevere to the end?

5. Why do we sometimes need to ask God for a willing spirit?

CONCLUSION

This week's Bible study reminds us that people don't change much in human history. The needs of the human heart remain rather constant over time. People come into this world with a preference toward self. They use free will to choose their own ways. They wake up one day deeper in sin than they realized was possible. More than anything else in the world, they need forgiveness for their acts of sinning and heart cleansing to take away the desire to sin. Thank God— He knows us better than we know ourselves; He provides two cleansings!

FOR FURTHER STUDY

Isa. 1:18; Ezek. 36:25-27; Mal. 3:3

My Consecration

Rom. 12:1-2

Book 1 of this Bible study series explained the Old Testament sacrificial system. No doubt, you wondered at times why a New Testament believer needs to know anything about rituals of the old covenant. After all, we live in the new covenant of Jesus Christ. Why waste time learning about outdated rituals from an ancient religion, right?

We believe this information is essential to understanding the meaning of the cross of Jesus Christ and how He made the atoning sacrifice for our sins. Jesus offered himself on the sacrificial altar just as so many animals had been offered on the altar for more than 1,000 years.

In this week's Bible study Paul uses a word picture that requires some understanding of the Old Testament sacrificial system. He talks about our consecration and provides an image of it as a sacrifice on the altar of the Tabernacle or Temple. With that ancient ritual in mind, let's approach this session's Bible lesson.

GROUP DISCUSSION

1. Why is it so important to believe the right doctrines about Christ?

2. Why must thinking correctly about sanctification precede an attempt to live a holy life?

READ ROM. 12:1-2

The first word of verse 1 signals a transition. Paul has spent the first eleven chapters of this book setting up a line of thought that begins to take practical application in chapter 12. The theological discussions in the earlier portions of the book as well as this practical application all speak of making Jesus the Lord of all of one's life. So we must believe the right doctrines about Christ, think correctly about our Christian faith, and live holy lives that honor God. Paul is now going to tell us how to position ourselves for success in holy living.

Paul reminds us to begin our consecration by remembering God's mercy in not condemning us in our sins but in giving us a second chance at living for Him. God's mercy becomes our motivation for consecration. In light of His mercy toward us, how should we respond? We should respond by offering our bodies as living sacrifices back to Him. Here's where the imagery of the Old Testament sacrificial system enters the picture. Worshippers brought live animals to the altar. But before the ritual ended, the priest took the animals' lives. They were no longer of earthly use since they died in the process of the sacrifice.

Paul says we should willingly place our bodies on the sacrificial altar. He intends more than just a dedication of our physical bodies; he implies all of our being as well. That is, we dedicate the physical, spiritual, emotional, and psychological parts of ourselves. God will not take our physical lives in the process; we will become living sacrifices. In other words, we consecrate our lives to God and His service—and then go on living.

GROUP DISCUSSION

1. Name all the ways God has been merciful to you.

2. Why does Paul's call to offer ourselves to God as a living sacrifice make sense?

3. How will this sacrifice change the way you live?

4. How will this sacrifice change your value system?

5. In what ways can a sacrifice that allows us to go on living be harder to make than one that requires the taking of our lives, as in dying for the sake of Christ?

Paul offers another window into this imagery through the sacrifice Jesus made for us on the Cross. That sacrifice cost Him His physical life. As His disciples, we should identify with Him in His consecration to the Father. Paul talked in Rom. 6:1-5 of our identifying with Christ in His death and resurrection. This identification takes the form of water baptism. In this ritual we die with Christ; God raises us to new life in Him.

In our Scripture lesson for today, we again identify with Christ. He willingly laid down His body to be nailed to the Cross. We, too, should willingly offer our lives back to God. Our consecration differs from Christ's in that we go on living following our act of dedication. His consecration required His life. Jesus reminded us in His earthly ministry that a servant is not greater than his master (Matt. 10:24). He climbed upon the sacrificial altar; we must follow.

PERSONAL REFLECTION

Take a moment and reflect on the notion that Christ is calling you to join Him in sacrificing your entire being to the Father, just as He did. In light of your love for Christ, what should your response be?

Some claim that Paul is admonishing prospective converts to the Christian faith. Thus, they say this consecration occurs at the time of a believer's conversion. The word "holy" in the middle of verse 1 indicates otherwise. Paul is addressing believers who have already been declared holy in light of the fact that they have invited Christ into their hearts. They are now, as holy ones, to offer themselves on the altar of sacrifice. This response pleases God. It is a response similar to the one Jesus experienced when He healed ten lepers. One returned to say, "Thank you," as His praise response to God (Luke 17:11-19). We praise God with our consecration.

GROUP DISCUSSION

1. What leads you to think that the timing of our consecration might occur after our repentance?

2. In what ways might our consecration be a thank offering to God?

In the last phrase of verse 1, Paul calls our consecration an act of worship. Worship in the Old Testament involved giving something to God. Today we usually think of giving Him our words of praise, our prayers, or our songs. But do those gifts really cost us anything? Perhaps we might say they cost us time and energy in going to a church building to offer them. Is that really much of a price to pay? On one particular occasion during his reign as king of Israel, David worshipped God by making a special sacrifice to Him. He gave us a principle that remains an important reminder to us today. He said, "I will not sacrifice to the LORD my God burnt offerings that cost me nothing" (2 Sam. 24:24). Ultimately, true worship always costs us something. Paul says in the last phrase of verse 1 that God is calling us to a type of worship that will cost us *everything*.

GROUP DISCUSSION

1. Why must worship of God be costly to be genuine?

2. Why does God ask for the full surrender of ourselves to Him?

Read Rom. 12:2 again. Once a person dies, he or she no longer has obligations to the law. A dead person no longer files an income tax form or registers to vote. In Paul's mind, believers who have offered themselves to God as living sacrifices are as good as dead while they live in this world. Therefore, they no longer think like the world thinks or value as the world values. They do not define reality the way most people define it. They do not need society to prescribe for them the latest in fashion, entertainment, or lifestyle choices. They march to the beat of a different drummer and have their sites set on different goals in life.

Believers consecrate themselves to God as living sacrifices, and something miraculous happens. They live by a different value system from the world; God performs a radical transformation in their lives. At times the transformation occurs so slowly that it's hardly perceivable—but real nonetheless. The transformation gives these consecrated believers the mind of Christ. Paul said in 1 Cor. 2:16, "We have the mind of Christ." We find ourselves placing a high value on the things Christ highly values. We lose interest in the things of the world that Christ tells us will pass away.

GROUP DISCUSSION

1. Give examples of ways of thinking that are important to the worldly minded but not important to Christ.

2. Give examples of things the world highly values but Christ does not value.

3. List ways Christians think and act as they develop the mind of Christ.

Offering ourselves as living sacrifices and developing the mind of Christ produce a very important result in our lives. We develop a sense of God's will. We do not follow His will begrudgingly or out of obligation. Rather, we discover that it's "good, pleasing and perfect," as Paul describes it. It's good because it comes from God; it's pleasing as we apply it to our lives; and it's perfect, not in the sense of perfect performance but in the sense of complete dedication to God. God accepts the offer of our lives and rewards us with an indescribable sense of His pleasure with us. What a priceless benefit of consecrated living!

PERSONAL REFLECTION

1. People often ask how it is possible to know God's will. How would you explain it to someone?

2. What benefits accrue to those who find and do God's will?

GROUP ACTIVITY

Give participants each a sheet of typing paper. Have them draw a graphic organizer of this Bible study. Encourage them to organize two sets of ideas on their papers: (1) what God does to bring about our salvation, and (2) what our responsibility is to live holy lives. Tell them to draw the ideas out with boxes and lines in a way that makes sense to them. Have them show their charts when all have completed the assignment.

FOR FURTHER STUDY

2 Tim. 2:21; Matt. 16:25; Matt. 19:21

FURTHER QUESTIONS

Take a moment at the conclusion of the session to encourage class participants to place their unanswered questions on note cards, along with this session number. They should then place their cards in an "odds and ends" box provided by the Bible study leader. Attention will be given to these questions in the last session of this study.

God's Gift of Sanctification

1 Thess. 4:1-8; 5:23-24

Just about every product you purchase for your home comes with an instruction guide. Everything from a new stereo system to a new toaster comes with its own manual. These owner's manuals always list the rules for the product's setup and operation. They also explain how the product should perform. When you see these products advertised on television or in the newspaper, you never see a factory worker reading a list of operational rules. Rather, you hear testimonials of satisfied customers singing the praises of this fine product. You're more likely to purchase one for yourself if you see the way the product works for real people than if you just hear how it's supposed to work.

That's the reason we're studying believers in the Thessalonian church this week. The Bible contains numerous references to the need for our sanctification and how it should theoretically operate in our lives. We'll probably have a clearer understanding of sanctification, however, if we just view a real-life application in the lives of real believers. The entire book of 1 Thess. deals with two important topics: the second coming of Christ and the call to holiness. The Bible often relates these two themes. Our study will focus on the second one.

READ 1 THESS. 4:1-8

Every believer must decide who he or she will please— God or self. Paul urges us in verse 1 to seek to please God in all we do. This is not just a suggestion made by a minister; it's a command coming from the authority of Jesus himself. Verse 3 zeros in on one of the two central themes of the book: "It is God's will that you should be sanctified."

So often believers pray for God's will in relation to their choice of a mate, a college, a career, or where to live. All important choices. None is more important, however, than seeking God's will for a clean and pure heart. None of the other choices will bring the satisfaction we seek in life if we do not first have hearts focused toward God.

GROUP DISCUSSION

1. Why should Christians live with a single purpose of seeking to please God, as referenced in 4:1?

2. Why is it important for us to differentiate between instructions we receive from other people and those we receive from God?

3. Which should be more important to us? Why?

4. Why does God desire our sanctification?

Paul first says our sanctification manifests itself in sexual purity. The Thessalonian Christians lived in a society plagued by sexual immorality. The prevailing culture condoned all sorts of sexual activity that the Bible condemned as sinful. Paul makes no implication of sexual immorality with the Thessalonians. He's urging them to resist all temptations to blend in with their culture and adopt its lax moral practices. He's urging them never to become comfortable with the world's moral standards; they must always remember that God calls them to a higher standard.

Verse 4 reminds us of an important responsibility: to learn to control ourselves. God may not take us out of temptation's reach, but He expects us to learn to say "No" to temptation's offers. Unbelievers live under the control of their passionate lusts; they surrender to temptation's suggestions. God expects more of believers. Holy living also mandates that we should never wrong or take advantage of others (v. 6).

GROUP DISCUSSION

1. How are believers today exposed to the same lax and immoral culture that the Thessalonians faced?

2. Give examples of immoral conduct presented as normal lifestyle choices in television, movies, music, magazines, and other media avenues.

3. What impact does society's influence have on you?

4. Is it hard to live a holy life in an unholy world? Why or why not?

5. What strategies work for you in resisting society's attempt to influence your value system and lifestyle choices?

6. How do we succeed over temptation's suggestions to us?

Verse 3 tells us it is God's will for us to be sanctified. Verse 7 tells us it is God's call to be holy. We find in verse 8 the means to make both of these a reality in our lives. The key to both God's will and God's call for our lives: God's gift to us, that is, the gift of His Holy Spirit. The tense of the verb indicates this is not a one-time gift but a continual, daily giving to us of His Spirit.

PERSONAL REFLECTION

Contemplate God's will and His call for your life with regard to holiness and sanctification. Now dwell on the fact that He is not asking you to reach this goal by yourself. He's offering you a gift to enable you to attain His goal for your life.

1. Do you feel a sense of relief that you're not expected to accomplish it by yourself?

2. What reaction do you have toward God for providing the means to accomplish His goal for you?

3. Offer a prayer to Him, telling Him how you feel about this gift He freely gives you.

READ 1 THESS. 5:23-24

Paul fills chapters 4 and 5 of this book with admonitions of things to do and not do in order to exemplify holiness. In 5:23-24 he suggests the secret that makes holiness possible in our lives. We can't discipline ourselves into such living. We just can't live up to the standard under our own power. We need the God of peace to do a work in our lives that will enable us to live up to His will and call on our lives. 1 Thess. 5:23 reminds us of the same truth found in 4:8, that is, that sanctification is not something we do for ourselves; rather, it's something God does for us. It's a gift from God that we receive by faith.

"To sanctify" means to set apart for God. God set apart the Tabernacle and Temple as places of worship in the Old Testament. He also set apart the instruments of worship. The New Testament references sanctification more for believers than things. God sets us apart for himself but with an added dimension. He cleanses and purifies our hearts and places His Holy Spirit within us to enable us to live the life to which He calls us.

"Blameless" does not imply "faultless." The word "blame" comes from the same word as "blaspheme," which means to deny that God is God. To be blameless is to be innocent of wrongdoing. In this context, it means to honor God as Lord of our lives. Faultless, on the other hand, means to be without error, to be flawless or perfect. Our hearts and motives can be blameless before God even though our actions may not always be flawless or perfect.

GROUP DISCUSSION

1. Think of examples of objects of worship found in the sanctuary where you worship that are set apart for the worship of God. Discuss them.

2. In what ways are believers set apart for God and His service?

3. What does God cleanse or purify from our hearts in sanctification?

4. Give examples of ways believers may be blameless but not faultless.

The verb "sanctify" in 5:23 differs significantly from the word "gives" in 4:8. In 4:8 Paul speaks of a continual, daily giving of His Spirit rather than a one-time gift. Think of a child receiving lunch money each day from Mom. In 5:23 Paul calls for a decisive action at a point in time. Think of receiving a birthday present from your parent. So, we see that God accepts our consecration, which we discussed in the previous Bible study on Rom. 12:1-2, by giving us the gift of sanctification at a moment in time. He also places His Holy Spirit in us on a daily basis. Hasn't His plan thought of everything!

God doesn't just do something to our religious nature or to our psychological nature. He does something to every part of our being: spirit, soul, and body. He touches every part of our spiritual and physical being. He gives to us; He sustains us. And how long does He sustain us? Until the newness wears from our spiritual experience or until we mature in our faith? No, He sustains us all the way to the second coming of Christ.

Paul wants to make sure we understand the source for fulfilling this call to holy living, so he reminds us of it again in 5:24. God is the one who calls; God is faithful; He will do it. Yes, my commitment to God is important. Yes, my self-discipline is important. However, God's gift of His Holy Spirit and His sanctification capture the real reasons any of us can live holy lives.

GROUP DISCUSSION

1. Think of an example of a gift that's given at a moment in time. Compare this to God's gift of sanctification.

2. Think of an example of a gift that keeps on giving over a long period of time. Compare this to God's daily gift of the presence of His Holy Spirit.

3. What is the significance of God's sanctifying every part of our being (spirit, soul, and body)?

5. How does it make you feel to realize that the promise of this passage is based not on your performance but on the faithfulness and power of God?

CONCLUSION

Paul's letter to the believers at Thessalonica reminds us of some important spiritual truths. We're all called to live holy lives. God's will and plan for our lives call for us to be sanctified. Sanctification comes to us as a gift from God. He sanctifies in a moment and gives His Spirit daily for a lifetime.

FOR FURTHER STUDY

James 4:8; 1 John 3:3; 1 Pet. 1:13-16

STUDY *8*

The Forerunner

Heb. 12:1-3, 11-14

Do you remember learning to tie your shoelaces? If you're a parent, do you remember teaching your children to tie their shoelaces? Do you remember reading an instruction manual on shoelace-tying? Of course not! Someone sits down with the child and guides him or her through the step-by-step process—not just once, but over and over until the skill is mastered. Even as an adult, I find I can learn a new skill much faster if someone shows me how to do it rather than reading about it in a book.

That's God's thought in our Scripture passage for this session. We've been looking at the Bible's call to holiness in this series of studies. We've seen our need for holiness and God's provision for meeting that need. But remember: a picture is worth a thousand words. We need someone to show us what a holy life *looks* like. We need an example to follow through a step-by-step process of how to live holiness on a daily basis. Heb. 12 gives us that picture.

GROUP DISCUSSION

Relate your experience of teaching someone a new skill, like tying shoelaces or a necktie. Address the following questions about that experience.

1. How did you go about teaching the skill? Did you just talk about the steps to be taken, or did you show the person?

2. What did you find most frustrating about the experience?

3. How many times did you have to demonstrate the skill before the person mastered it?

4. What did you find most rewarding about the experience?

READ HEB. 12:1

Heb. 12 forms an analogy. It pictures the Christian life as a long-distance race rather than a short sprint. Believers run in the race. The Bible heroes of Heb. 11 have raced before us. They have finished the race, and now they sit in the grandstands watching and cheering us on. They serve as inspiring examples of keeping the faith through every obstacle. They witness to us about God's faithfulness to the runners. But more than that, their *witness* for Christ sometimes led to their *martyrdom*. The victory and reward of completing the race proved in the long run to be worth the price it cost them.

We must follow that example. Just like any good runner, we must throw off everything that might slow us down. We toss aside any actions, habits, or lifestyles that hinder a holy life. We free ourselves from extra weight and unnecessary baggage. Sin represents the heaviest weight of all; we discard it in all of its forms. No list of sins follows this admonition, because Satan has an almost infinite capacity to appeal to us with one temptation or another. He tempts each of us in different ways. Regardless of the temptation, it gets the same negative response from us.

To persevere means to stand our ground or endure. We're not programmed to inevitably yield to temptation. Satan would like for us to believe otherwise. He wants us to think of sin as inevitable. We might as well yield to temptation in the morning rather than in the afternoon, because one way or another we will yield. We might as well yield now and enjoy ourselves! Don't give in to this wrong thinking. Other runners have gone before us on this journey of faith and have stood their ground against temptation; so can we.

We're not left to figure out the race lanes for ourselves. They're clearly marked. No guessing game here. God clearly marks the holiness path. We must decide if we want to take the high route of holiness. If we decide that we want to take that route, we're in good company.

GROUP DISCUSSION

1. Think of as many comparisons as you can to link the Christian life to a long-distance race.

2. Why do you think God gave us examples to follow for this life of holiness?

3. Name some hindrances to the life of holiness that are not necessarily sinful in and of themselves.

4. In what ways does sin become a weight on us that hinders our progress as Christians?

5. What have you found to be the best techniques for resisting temptation?

6. Where do we find the markers for this clearly marked path described in verse 1?

READ HEB. 12:2-3

You've probably been to concerts where a lesser-known musician comes out ahead of the headliner to "warm up" the audience. In Heb. 12:2-3, the writer presents the example of the great grandstand of witnesses who have finished the race before us. But they're not the best example; they're the warm-up act. The best example comes in verse 2. Of all the Bible heroes of faith, Jesus tops them all! He's run this race before us, and He finished it in tremendous victory.

Look closely at verse 2. Jesus designed this race of faith, so He's the author of it. He also ran it perfectly, so He knows how it feels to suffer, ache from head to toe, and endure the weary miles. In other words, Jesus can sympathize with weary runners because He's been there and done that. He understands your situation along the path. He's telling you, "It can be done," because He did it! It's significant that the Bible refers to our Savior as Jesus. That name reminds us of the human side of Jesus Christ, the side that was tempted in every way as we are. Yet He did not sin (Heb. 4:15).

What motivated Him to run the race? Look again at verse 2: "the joy set before him." What was that joy? Was it heaven itself? No, He had been there from eternity past and would return to His home. He found joy in bringing about *our* salvation and thus bringing us to heaven to live with Him. See Heb. 2:10 for another reference to this concept. Imagine that—His *joy* was *our* salvation! If Jesus was motivated by *my* salvation to run this race of holiness clear through to the finish line, shouldn't I be motivated as well?

Jesus endured the Cross for our salvation. He endured

much more than physical suffering. He also endured the social shame attached to this form of death. Government officials performed crucifixions only on terrible criminals and social outcasts. Through all the pain and humiliation, Jesus saw your salvation and mine—the result of His sacrifice. After completing the race of faith, Jesus "sat down at the right hand of the throne of God." This represents His eternal position of authority as the Son of God.

You and I must keep our eyes fixed on Jesus, because He expects us to do what He did. That is, we must endure all opposition, not grow weary, and never lose heart. Runners may be tempted to fall by the wayside and give up on the race. But Jesus did not give up, and neither should we. His victory over every obstacle remains the pattern for our victory.

GROUP DISCUSSION

1. What makes Jesus the best example for this race of faith?

2. How does it help you to know that Jesus was tempted just as you are?

3. Give examples of how you set a motivating symbol in a significant place to remind you of a goal you're striving toward.

4. In what ways can you set your eternal salvation before you as a motivating symbol to remind you to strive on?

5. In what ways do you suffer as a believer for the sake of Christ?

In verses 4-10 the author talks about God's discipline in our lives and our struggles against sin and temptation. This passage contains enough material for an entire Bible study session. In the interest of time, we must skip to verses 11-14 to complete the thought of this session's Bible study.

READ HEB. 12:11-14

Feeble arms and weak knees picture tired runners, weary in well-doing and ready to fall by the wayside. It's much easier to quit when you're dead tired and can't see the finish line. Strength for us weary Christian runners comes from keeping our eyes fixed on Jesus, the One who has blazed the path before us. We must put in perspective the discipline described in verses 4-11. God finds ways to work it all together to bring about righteousness and peace in our lives (v. 11). Righteousness speaks of God helping us do the right thing in varying circumstances; peace, referring to health and wholeness, comes from God and brings well-being to us as we perform right acts.

Level paths, also translated straight tracks, picture runners staying on the marked path. They don't venture off into the woods or onto a side road. It often takes a great deal of effort to stick to the straight path rather than go the way of least resistance, which can take us in any number of directions. The image also pictures making every effort to level the path when necessary, because other runners will come behind you. We don't want weaker or lame believers being tripped up or disabled because we left them with the example of an uneven path. It's not just our spiritual growth that's at stake here—others follow right behind us.

Again, this path remains straight as we keep our eyes fixed on Jesus. When I was a child I learned an important lesson about keeping a row straight when planting crops in a large field. You never look down at the ground. You always spot a tree at the end of the field and head straight toward it. When you reach that tree and look back, you'll see a straight row. In the same way, we're to spot Jesus, then head straight toward Him.

Verse 11 teaches us that holiness and peace go hand-in-hand. One leads to the other. This life of holiness encompasses all that God does for us from the moment He saves us from our sins and changes our lifestyles through growth in grace and sanctification clear up to the time we go to live with Him forever. Remember: the path of holiness ultimately leads to meeting the Lord face to face.

GROUP DISCUSSION

1. Have you ever felt like giving up on the race of faith?

2. What brought you to that point?

3. How did you get beyond that low point in your spiritual life?

4. Why does the Bible make a connection between righteousness and peace?

5. What are some of the side paths that can detour believers from the straight, marked path?

6. How do we resist the temptation to take some of those side paths?

7. Why is it important to remember that other believers follow closely behind us and follow our lead in this race?

8. List all the concepts the author might include in the broad concept of holiness found in verse 14 that lead us to seeing the Lord.

GROUP ACTIVITY

Bible study leader, write out 10 questions and answers from this week's material. Place each question on a note card; place each answer on a different card. Mix the cards. Have class participants match the questions with the correct answers to review the important points of this study. [Large study groups will need several sets of cards so the large group may be divided into smaller groups for this activity.]

FOR FURTHER STUDY

Heb. 11:2-38; Matt. 11:29; Matt. 16:24; John 13:15; Heb. 3:1; 1 Pet. 2:21

Our Coach

1 John 1:5—2:6

The prominent theme of last week's Bible study—fixing our eyes on Jesus—leads into the main thought of this week's study. The last verse of our passage this week says, "Whoever claims to live in him must walk as Jesus did" (1 John 2:6). In other words, we're urged in this passage to follow the same line of action we learned about last week. That is, fix our eyes on Jesus and run in His direction, living and walking in His example. Last week's study focused on Jesus as our forerunner. This week's study pictures Jesus as one who runs *beside* us, coaching us along. The One who successfully completed the race came back to run alongside us and coach us to the finish line.

GROUP DISCUSSION

Last week we used the analogy of believers as runners in the race of faith. Think now of Jesus as the coach, running along with us and giving us directions we can use to successfully complete the race.

1. Which image seems more personal to you: Jesus at the finish line calling for you to strive onward or Jesus as a coach, running alongside you?

2. Why do long-distance running coaches often run alongside their student athletes?

3. What spiritual lessons can you learn from this image even before we begin a study of the Scripture passage?

READ 1 JOHN 1:5-7

John got his message straight from Jesus, who got it from firsthand experience with the Father in heaven. So John feels confident about the accuracy of his message. The first image of God that he gives relates to His holiness. The image of God as light references His purity and holiness. Since darkness represents sin, God dwells in the absence of it.

We live in a day when people want to portray everyone with both a good and a bad side. Movies frequently show the dark side of an otherwise good character and the virtuous side of an evil character. Our society teaches children to look for the good in everyone, even people they might think of as bad characters. John would see this cohabitation of good and bad in the same person as impossible, because he sees the matter in terms of light and darkness. When light fills a room, darkness disappears. God dwells in total light without a hint of a dark corner.

GROUP DISCUSSION

1. Name popular movies or television programs that portray characters as having both good and bad sides.

2. Why does the Bible frequently portray God as living in complete light?

3. What does that teach you about Him?

The second image John gives indicates that Christians don't make a practice of sinning. The thrust of verses 6 and 7 indicates an habitual practice of sinful acts or attitudes, not an occasional stumble or a falling short. We can't claim to be Christian and continue practicing sin. A sinful lifestyle can never be compatible with a Christian confession of faith. Fellowship with God implies walking in the light of honesty and openness before God. That calls for more than doing good deeds; it requires living in truth. No room remains for a secret or false life lived in the dark shadows of the night.

The third image John gives in this passage places us in daily fellowship both with God and other believers. At the same time, the blood of Jesus Christ continues to cleanse us from all sin. The original root of the word for "purifies" gives us the image of sin being continually burned out of our hearts, the way a surgeon cauterizes a bleeding blood vessel. All the verbs in this verse are in the present tense—*every day* as we live in constant fellowship with Jesus Christ.

GROUP DISCUSSION

1. Why is a lifestyle of sinning incompatible with daily fellowship with Jesus Christ?

2. How would you use this passage of Scripture to reason with a believer who claimed to be following Christ while at the same time living a sinful lifestyle?

3. John connects our fellowship with God to the blood of Jesus Christ purifying us from all sin. What is the connection between these two concepts?

READ 1 JOHN 1:8-10

John speaks of sin (singular) and *not* sins (plural) in verse 8. He refers to the nature with which every child of Adam and Eve comes into the world—a nature focused on itself, a nature programmed to prefer its own way. We all are born with such a nature, and no amount of denying that fact will change anything. Denying it is nothing less than self-deception.

So what is our hope? Our *only* hope is to confess our sins to God and plead for His grace and mercy. If we accept God's offer, we can count on His faithfulness to us to do two essential things: forgive us for our acts of sinning and purify us from our sinful nature. At no point can we brag about our accomplishments in this process. At no time do we achieve superior spirituality. Our salvation—from the very start—is the result of God's grace.

PERSONAL REFLECTION

1. Think about your own life. When did you first realize you had a sinful nature, urging you to go your own way and do your own thing?

2. When you began to realize a sinful nature dwelt in your heart, did you openly admit it or try to deny the fact?

3. If you denied it, did that denial take away the negative influence of this sinful nature?

4. God has offered you forgiveness of your sins and purification of your heart for the asking. Have you taken Him up on His offer? Why or why not?

5. Why can we not brag or claim superior spirituality once God forgives and purifies us?

6. Can you think of ways one might brag or claim superior spirituality?

7. What is the best method for avoiding this trap?

READ 1 JOHN 2:1

John refers to his readers in a close, personal way. He's not just making theological statements; they're words of advice on how to live daily life. John states his goal clearly: to avoid sin. Is he dangling bait before us, intending to trick us? Is this goal unrealistic and unattainable? No way! Freedom from sin is a real possibility. It's not that we're taken out of the realm of possibility for sinning but that our fellowship with God and other believers gives us the possibility to avoid it.

What if a believer does fall back into sin? God's grace comes running to meet us at the point of our failure and coaches us back to the heart of God. This grace is not impersonal; it's quite personal in the form of our Savior, Jesus himself. He's the one who pleads our case to the Father and speaks in our defense. John's reference to the rescue plan for a believer who falls back in sin comes in the form of an emergency door on an airplane rather than a turnstile at the entrance of an amusement park. In other words, it's available if necessary but certainly not for daily practice.

GROUP DISCUSSION

1. Why does our society look on the possibility of living a sinless lifestyle as unrealistic or unattainable?

2. Why do many people have this belief?

3. Are you convinced that John is calling for us to live sin-free? Why or why not?

4. What's the difference in viewing this passage as an emergency door on an airplane rather than a turnstile at the entrance of an amusement park?

READ 1 JOHN 2:2

Not only does Jesus plead our case before the Father, as a lawyer would do before a judge, but He also makes the atoning sacrifice for our sins. We spent time in studies 9, 10, and 11 of Book 1 of this Bible study series talking about Jesus' sacrifice of himself on the Cross to atone for our sins. The imagery of 1 John 2:2 pictures the mercy seat in the Old Testament (Exod. 37:1-9). The mercy seat refers to the top of the

Ark of the Covenant located in the Holy of Holies of the Tabernacle and the Temple. God dwelt there in glory. The high priest placed the blood of sacrificial bulls and goats on the mercy seat on the Day of Atonement (Lev. 16). Once the blood covered the mercy seat, God and humanity could meet for sins' forgiveness. Our sins disappear from the record as we once again enjoy fellowship with God, hence the term "at-one-ment," or "atonement." Christ can represent our case to the Father because He has paid the price required for our sins to be removed from us.

PERSONAL REFLECTION

Has this additional insight affected your feelings toward Jesus? Not only does He run alongside you to coach you in your race of faith, not only does He represent your case to the Father, but He is also the One who, without our even asking, personally paid the price for our atonement with God.

READ 1 JOHN 2:3-6

If we truly believe in Jesus Christ, we continually obey and follow Him. We keep His commands; His truth abides in us. God's love finds completion in us. 1 John 2:3-6 outlines the way a lifestyle of holiness looks in a believer. We walk, talk, and live as Jesus did. We end this study where it began: "Whoever claims to live in him must walk as Jesus did" (v. 6)

GROUP DISCUSSION

1. This passage admonishes us to continually obey and follow Christ. How do we know what He wants us to do on a daily basis?

2. What do we mean when we say God's love finds completion in us?

3. People often talk about how complicated holiness is. This passage says holiness is walking, talking, and living as Jesus did. What's complicated about that?

GROUP ACTIVITY

Close your time together by discussing the various images of Christ discussed in this session. Give the Bible study participants note cards. Encourage them to write about the image of Christ that helps them most and the reasons why. Ask them not to write their names on the cards. When everyone has completed the task, the group leader will take up the cards and read them to the entire group.

FOR FURTHER STUDY

Luke 18:16; 1 Pet. 2:2; Heb. 9:15, 24

FURTHER QUESTIONS

Take a moment at the conclusion of the session to encourage class participants to place their unanswered questions on note cards, along with this session number. They should then place their cards in an "odds and ends" box provided by the Bible study leader. Attention will be given to these questions in the last session of this study.

Life in the Spirit

Rom. 8:1-17

Talk about a goldmine of insight into holy life! Rom. 8 contains more good information than we could possibly introduce in one brief Bible study. In fact, entire books have been written just to unpack the rich insights of this one chapter. Life lived under the Holy Spirit's influence captures the essence of living the holy life.

READ ROM. 8:1

The "therefore" of Rom. 8:1 refers back to the condemnation of the law explored in chapter 7. Christ took your place and mine on the Cross; therefore He freed us from sin. As we discussed in last week's Bible study, Christ has made us "at one" with the Father by covering our sins with His blood. We don't need to wait for death to bring our deliverance from the bondage of sin. That deliverance becomes a present reality as we walk in the Spirit. The key to understanding this session's Scripture passage lies at the end of verse 1. The incredible freedom of which Paul speaks requires us to make a conscious daily choice between two alternative ways of thinking, valuing, and living. We will spend most of the rest of the study of this passage comparing and contrasting these two alternatives. Way One lives life pleasing the flesh; Way Two lives life pleasing the Spirit.

PERSONAL REFLECTION

How does it make you feel to realize that because you have accepted Jesus Christ as your personal Savior, you can live your life on earth completely free from divine condemnation?

READ ROM. 8:2-9

Verses 2-9 clearly differentiate between life in the flesh and life in the Spirit. Paul refers to the flesh more than 12 times and the Spirit 16 times in our Bible lesson for this session. Rather than studying this section verse by verse, we'll study the contrasts offered between flesh and Spirit. References will be offered with each contrast to connect the ideas back to Scripture. The following are Paul's observations on the two ways of living:

1. Two preferences (8:1, 9)

A. *In Christ Jesus.* We are in Christ; He is in us. The Spirit of God brings the living presence of Christ not just *to* us but *in* us. We are united with Him in a mystical connection that brings daily communion between our spirits and His Spirit. Our spirits are not absorbed by His so as to nullify our personhood or cancel our free will. We still make choices and think our own thoughts. The difference centers on our wills preferring God's will to the point that His will becomes the very oxygen we breathe.

B. *In the flesh.* The Bible uses flesh in three main ways: (1) our bodies, (2) the human point of view, and (3) the carnal nature of humanity that prefers self over God. Paul intends the third way in this passage of Scripture. The flesh represents a world that makes no attempt to please or prefer God. It does what it wants, when it wants, and in the manner it wants. It follows imagination's every whim and seeks it own happiness over other priorities.

PERSONAL REFLECTION

Which of these two preferences do you choose? Why?

2. Two walks (8:1, 4-5, 9)

A. *Fleshly walk.* This walk stays in step with the music of the world's value system. Self-will, self-seeking, and self-gratification mark the path for this walk. Sometimes the path goes over other people's backs, feelings, or well-being, but no matter—self preference always carries the most authority in marking out the trail. The intention may not be to totally disregard God's ways, just to avoid letting His ways take preference over our own ways.

B. *Spiritual walk.* This walk keeps in step with the music of God's value system. Self-will falls along the roadside as the will and preference of God mark out the path for this walk. Sometimes this path runs totally counter to what we might choose for ourselves, but never mind. We want God's will so passionately that preferences we might have for ourselves don't seem that important in light of His plans for us.

PERSONAL REFLECTION

Which of these two walks do you choose? Why?

3. Two laws (8:2)

A. *The law of the Spirit of life.* This law does not come from a rulebook or court bench but from the heart of Christ. It guides our thinking, feelings, actions, and attitudes. It's not so much a list of dos and don'ts as it is the boundary lines of the relationship we have with God. That love relationship with God causes us to long for His ways, as taught to us by His Spirit.

B. *The law of death.* This law comes from Satan. It tells us, "Anything goes. Do what you please. Look out for Number One." It's a law that disregards all law. "Think what you want to think. Do whatever you want to do. Treat others any way you like. Make yourself happy." So, what's the problem with this law? It leads straight into the jaws of death.

PERSONAL REFLECTION

Which of these two laws do you choose? Why?

4. Two powers (8:3-4)

A. *The power of the Ten Commandments.* This law tells us that we must follow every regulation precisely to please God. However, it's humanly impossible to keep every regulation precisely. So when we fail or fall short, this law condemns us. It offers no power to succeed or further hope that we can ever meet its demands. Like a taskmaster who cannot be pleased, it tells us we're wrong but offers no plan for correcting our ways.

B. *The power of Christ.* Christ became our representative on the Cross. By His sacrifice we now have full remission for our sins. In God's eyes, it's just as if we had never sinned in the first place. There's a big difference between God's forgiving—but remembering—our sins and God's forgiving and forgetting our sins. He does the latter. Christ's power gives us a new heart toward God and a new start with Him. Amazing power!

PERSONAL REFLECTION

Which of these two powers do you choose? Why?

5. Two loyalties (8:5)

A. *Loyalty to the flesh.* This loyalty subjects us to the powerful whims of our desires, our addictions, and our passions. We become slaves to every lowly, fallen drive that enters our depraved mind. We don't obey them because we think they're best for us. We just can't help ourselves! Loyalty to the flesh defies logic or reason. It needs no other argument than "because I want to."

B. *Loyalty to the Spirit.* This loyalty subjects us to the directives of the Spirit. It aims us toward God's will and preferences. Our desires fall subject to God's holy, pure, and good desires for us. It's not that we long to do one thing but force ourselves to do something else. It's that our desires conform to His to the point that more than anything else in the world, we want what He wants. Our pleasure is to do His pleasure.

PERSONAL REFLECTION

Which of these two loyalties do you choose? Why?

6. Two destinies (8:6-7)

A. *Death.* As discussed with "the law of death," the end of this path leads to total and final destruction. The final stage of addiction brings total bondage. The final stage of self-seeking brings total selfishness. The final stage of the life of the flesh brings physical, spiritual, psychological, and emotional death.

B. *Life.* It's quite ironic. Jesus said that to save your life, you lose it (Matt. 16:25). So when you surrender your will, preferences, desires, hopes, dreams, plans, wishes, body, soul, and spirit to God's Spirit, rather than losing your life, you actually gain life to the fullest. We need not wait for the end of our journeys on earth to enjoy eternal life. Life lived in the Spirit gives us the joys and benefits of eternal life right now.

PERSONAL REFLECTION

Which of these two destinies do you choose? Why?

GROUP ACTIVITY

Have two members of the group each prepare a persuasive speech to give during the Bible study session. One class member will give all of the positive features of life in the flesh. The other class member will give all of the positive features of life in the Spirit. Each will attempt to persuade the group that their way is the best way to live. After the presentations, have class members discuss why each way has advocates.

ROM. 8:10-17

In Romans 8, Paul contrasts two ways of living and declares that believers have no condemnation from God. He outlines the glorious benefits of life in the Spirit.
- The Spirit of God dwelling in our hearts (v. 10)
- Physical resurrection from the dead (v. 11)
- Adoption into the family of God (vv. 14-15)
- The witness of God's Spirit to our spirit (v. 16)
- Being joint-heirs with Christ (v. 17)
- Glorification in heaven (v. 17)

GROUP DISCUSSION

1. Which benefits of life in the Spirit do you most enjoy today?

2. Which benefits of life in the Spirit do you most look forward to in the future?

3. With such a clear-cut distinction drawn between these two ways, why would anyone choose to miss life in the Spirit?

FOR FURTHER STUDY

Gal. 5:16-26; Rom. 8:26-39; 1 Cor. 2:10-16

Growing in the Spirit

Col. 1:9-12; Eph. 4:11-16

I once lived in a house with a tree in its front yard that had a strange problem. All the trees in the other front yards on our block stood 30 to 40 feet tall and had wide, sweeping branches. Our little tree measured only 10 feet tall and had just a few scrawny branches. Was I justified in comparing my little tree to the other trees in the neighborhood? Of course I was! A developer had planted all the trees on our street at the same time more than 20 years earlier. But my little tree had failed to thrive because our yard had a solid rock shelf just below the surface of the lawn. The rock prevented my tree from developing the root system necessary for healthy growth.

Babies bring joy and satisfaction to families the world over. Almost everything about the baby stage of life is exciting—for a season. But we wouldn't want the baby stage to last 10 or 15 years, would we? God programs every living thing on earth to grow and develop. Growth naturally follows life. That rule holds true for *spiritual* life as well. The passages of Scripture for this session offer important insights into God's plan for our spiritual development.

GROUP DISCUSSION

1. Think about the "baby stage" of life. What do you enjoy most about it?

2. What do you enjoy least about it?

3. What would you think about a child who never grew out of that stage of life?

4. What do babies growing up and Christians growing up have in common?

READ COL. 1:9-12

God grants us the incredible gift of spiritual life. But we're not just passive recipients. He expects us to do our part, so to speak, in order to exercise, grow, and mature in our spiritual lives. Col. 1:9-12 reminds us that we need to be continually filled with an awareness of God's will. As we intentionally study God's Word and purposefully participate in the spiritual exercises that develop us, we grow in spiritual wisdom and understanding. Our spiritual journeys may begin in a rush of feeling and emotion that will eventually subside. We never find a solid foundation for our spiritual journeys in feeling and emotion. We must move on to spiritual wisdom and understanding for solid growth.

Such wisdom and understanding lead to responsible living. Our faith bears fruit in the daily conduct of godly living that pleases Him. Notice how wisdom and understanding lead to good works. We always live out what we believe. That's why it's so important to believe biblical truth. Growth in wisdom, understanding, and good works lead to growth in our knowledge of God.

We in turn find new strength from God for endurance, patience, and joyful thanksgiving: all signs of Christian maturity. Paul reminds us again of our heavenly inheritance at the culmination of our spiritual journeys. From now until that day, we live as citizens of the kingdom of light. Recall from Study 9 our analysis of this analogy. Light symbolizes holiness, righteousness, truth, and life. All belong to us because we belong to Him.

GROUP DISCUSSION

1. List as many parental admonitions as you can think of related to the rules and regulations for childhood growth and development. (Examples: Eat your vegetables. Get plenty of rest. Drink your milk.)

2. List as many biblical admonitions as you can think of for assisting spiritual growth and development. (Examples: Read the Bible. Pray. Attend church regularly.)

3. How do we nurture a continual awareness of God's will in our lives?

4. What is the connection or relationship between what we believe and how we live?

5. Why is this connection so direct?

6. What are some of the benefits of living as a citizen in the kingdom of light?

READ EPH. 4:11-13

In Book 3 we'll consider Eph. 4:11-13 again from a different perspective. At this point in our study, notice God's plan and provision for our spiritual growth and development. Verse 11 lists the workers He calls to instruct and encourage His followers. Why does He do this for us? Notice the reasons listed in the following verses:

- To prepare us for works of service (v. 12)
- To build up the body of Christ (v. 12)
- To bring unity in the faith (v. 13)
- To bring unity in the knowledge of Jesus (v. 13)
- To bring spiritual maturity (v. 13)

From this we can see God's plan to enrich our lives personally as well as to enrich the community of faith. We grow as we minister to one another, and the community of faith also grows as we minister. All are strengthened and helped as we develop both individually and corporately.

What's the purpose of this plan? It's to bring us to a common belief, a common Savior, and a common model for our spiritual maturity.

GROUP DISCUSSION

1. What works of service is God calling you to do?

2. In what ways does God wish to build up the body of Christ in which you participate?

3. What does unity in the faith mean to you?

4. What does unity in the knowledge of Jesus mean to you?

5. What do you think you'll look like when you're spiritually mature?

READ EPH. 4:14-16

Paul presents in verses 14-16 the alternative to God's plan and goal for us. God doesn't want us to be spiritual babies, infants that never grow out of the "baby stage." He doesn't want us to be like little life rafts floating aimlessly on open seas. These are the images of believers who do not move on to Christian maturity. The winds that blow them around are the false teachings that waft through society, media, and sometimes even the Church. At times false teachings can blow through unintentionally. That is, sometimes people innocently throw out false ideas for consideration without a motive. At other times, though, false teachers intentionally target certain believers with the specific goal of leading them astray. Spiritual growth and maturity insulate believers from these pitfalls.

If God has His way in us, we'll speak and hear the truth, and we'll grow up in Christ. Christ works like glue, holding believers together to form His body on earth. The last portion of this passage still has us growing. We build each other up in love; we each do our part to help and support one another. Christian maturity brings spiritual unity to the body of Christ.

GROUP DISCUSSION

1. What images come to mind as you picture believers either as perpetual infants or little life rafts floating aimlessly on open seas?

2. Name some of the false teachings that blow through society, media, and the Church.

3. What makes them false teachings?

4. How do you know they're false?

5. What prevents you from being led astray by these false teachings?

6. Why do false teachers intentionally target certain believers with the intention of leading them astray?

7. This passage calls us to continual spiritual growth. What's the alternative?

CONCLUSION

Passages of Scripture such as the ones we've studied today and the ones listed below for further study remind us that God steers us away from spiritual complacency in our lives. We must never relax our efforts toward further growth by feeling that we have arrived spiritually. We must never think that right standing with God exempts us from the need for further spiritual growth. We must balance our thinking between satisfaction in what Christ accomplished for us on the Cross and the need to press forward to a deeper walk with God. We can relax our efforts only after we step through the gates of our heavenly home.

GROUP ACTIVITY

Have someone in the group role-play an adult who never grew up. This individual can talk and act like a little child. Make it a time of fun at the end of this Bible study session.

Have the group close this session by listing ways we press on in our faith toward maturity so no one gets left behind as a childish believer.

FOR FURTHER STUDY

1 Cor. 13:11; 14:20; Heb. 5:14; 6:1; 1 John 2:14; 1 Pet. 2:2; 2 Pet. 1:5-6

Tying It All Together

We started this book with the idea that God's plan for His children to live holy lives carries over from the Old Testament to the New Testament. We discovered that not only did He maintain this desire in the New Testament but also this desire increased to include more facets of our lives than the Old Testament considered.

Our study of holiness in the New Testament dealt primarily with individual holiness, hence the title of this book, *The Journey Within.* Our study brought God's will and plan for our lives into sharper focus. We saw Him at work, often behind the scenes, setting the stage and making every necessary provision for us to successfully pursue His will and plan for us.

We want to take time at the end of this particular study to review what we've already studied and answer any questions that may remain in students' thinking. We'll begin this week's study with a group discussion of unanswered questions.

GROUP ACTIVITY

Bible study participants have been encouraged throughout this study to place their unanswered questions on note cards in the "odds and ends" box. Use time at the beginning of this session to consider the answers to these questions in the form of a group discussion. The Bible study leader should add clarity wherever necessary and draw each question, with answers, to a close. It's very possible that more time will be needed to adequately address lingering questions than one study session can accommodate. In that case, plan ahead to make this study a two-part session. It's important that all previous questions be answered before moving on to a final wrap-up of the study material.

READ MATT. 5:48

We began this Bible study with these words of Jesus from the Sermon on the Mount. Make no mistake about it—Jesus calls us to a life of holiness. His call seems a bit far-fetched. I mean, come on—get real! Be as perfect as God? The goal seems unattainable. *Unless*, that is, His words signal a promise rather than a command. Too often people write off these words of Jesus as a hopelessly unreachable goal. Then they do not feel responsible for them. It just may be that Jesus' promise places the words back within our reach as we realize that God looks at our hearts, our intentions, our motives, and our desires for the standard of perfection. From this perspective, holiness is more about relationship with God than perfect performance. It's more about a vital union of our spirits with His Spirit.

GROUP DISCUSSION

How does your perspective on Jesus' words change as you shift the emphasis of perfection from performance to your heart, your intentions, your motives, and your desires?

READ JOHN 14:15-16

When we sit down and contemplate this journey with God, fear and uncertainty can enter the picture. How can we possibly navigate a journey with the Creator of the universe? Sounds a little absurd, doesn't it?

I'm the family member responsible for trip details for our family vacations. When planning our annual vacation, I spend hours gathering information on various locations, calling airlines and motels, and finalizing trip details. The task seems overwhelming at times.

John 14:15-16 reminds us that we're not alone on this adventure with God. We don't plan and execute the trip by ourselves. He's provided a Counselor to live within our hearts and direct us every step of the way. You might say He's a personal navigator for the journey.

PERSONAL REFLECTION

Think for a moment about the personal direction the Holy Spirit offers to you on a daily basis. Breathe a prayer of thanks for His help. Ask Him to help you discover ways to use His help more effectively. Seek His direction for a specific problem you face.

READ ACTS 1:8

Something radical happened in the lives of Jesus' disciples on the Day of Pentecost. They enjoyed the good fortune of attending God's initial birthday celebration for the Church. What God did in the hearts of those first disciples He eagerly waits to do in our hearts as well. We see the blessed baptism with the Holy Spirit coming later to disciples in Acts 8, 10, and 19. So we know from these other examples that Pentecost was not just a one-time event. We need our own *personal* Pentecost to have our hearts prepared for our journeys with God. We must know the Holy Spirit in His fullness.

GROUP DISCUSSION

Why is the baptism with the Holy Spirit a necessary event in the life of every believer who wants an adventure with God?

READ PS. 51:10-12

David realized from personal experience that he needed heart cleansing more than anything else in the world. In our study of this passage, we noted that the word "cleanse" literally means "un-sin." Only God can do this, because only a divine washing of our inner nature will solve our problem with a depraved nature. Only God can change us from the inside out with His inner transformation. We see again in this passage that God provides everything necessary for us to make this journey with Him.

GROUP DISCUSSION

Why is heart cleansing such an important component of each individual's journey with God?

READ ROM. 12:1-2

A life of holiness always begins by acknowledging our total dependence on God. He devised the plan; He provides everything necessary for us to live in vital union with Him. We're not passive participants, however. He calls upon us for important involvement in this journey. We open ourselves to His work of heart cleansing. Then we consecrate ourselves back to Him for service. This consecration represents an act of worship. We become living sacrifices for Him.

GROUP DISCUSSION

What does a living sacrifice do on a daily basis to maintain this perspective on life, God, and self?

READ 1 THESS. 5:23-24

The spotlight shifts back to God in 1 Thess. 5:23-24 as we again consider what He does for us to prepare us for our adventure with Him. Rom. 12:1-2 speaks of what *we* do; this passage speaks of what *God does for us.* Sanctification can be received only as a gift of faith. It's never earned or deserved. The thrust of this message focuses on the willingness and adequacy of God. He remains faithful; He will do it.

PERSONAL REFLECTION

1. How does it help you to realize that sanctification is a gift from God rather than something you earn through your own efforts?

2. In what way do you have a sense of relief from trying to do it on your own?

READ HEB. 12:1-3

God thought of everything! Not only does He devise the plan for our adventure with Him, but He also provides everything necessary for us to follow that plan. In Heb. 12:1-3 we see that He even gives us a role model to follow. Jesus Christ helps us in a number of ways. He provides us with an example. He scouts out the trail ahead of us. He finishes the race. Then He comes back to coach us along the path to assure our victory. Yes, God thought of everything.

GROUP DISCUSSION

What have you discovered to be the best way to keep your eyes fixed on Jesus as a thousand sights and sounds come at you each day to distract you?

READ ROM. 6:1-2

In Rom. 8:1-2 Paul marks out two paths for us. Each offers a totally different way of approaching life; each ends at a very different destination. Like it or not, you walk on one of these paths. So you might as well choose the path that leads you to where you want to go. Without a doubt, life in the Spirit offers the best path for a variety of reasons. It's not an easy path. It will cost you everything. Jesus referred to it in terms of losing your life (Matt. 16:25). But at the end of the journey you'll realize you chose the path that leads to eternal life. This adventure with God encompasses a journey not only for life on earth but for eternal life as well. What an awesome adventure!

GROUP DISCUSSION

In your own words, describe what it means to walk in life with the Spirit.

FINAL GROUP ACTIVITY

Break the class into pairs. Have these pairs share their responses to each of these questions. Then have one member of each pair share the high points of their discussion with the entire group.

1. What has been your greatest insight about "the journey within" from this Bible study?

2. What has been the hardest concept for you to grasp in this Bible study?

3. What is your favorite passage of Scripture from this Bible study?

4. How has your life changed as a result of this Bible study?

MOVING ON

Our adventure with God doesn't stop with understanding God's plan (Book 1) and the individual journey (Book 2). There's more—a lot more. In the next book (Book 3) of this Bible study series we'll consider our adventure with God from the perspective of "traveling with friends." In this book we'll learn how to live the life of holiness in the Christian community and in our troubled world. People often end their study of holiness with the individual's perspective. Join us as we continue our exploration of God's incredible journey with His children.